People of Discount Stores Coloring Book

Hi everyone,

Thank you so much for purchasing this coloring book. I hope you enjoy it!

I have a special surprise for you…

Claim your gift here: https://bit.ly/2K58AtH

Thanks so much and happy coloring!

© 2018 Maria Walmen

All Rights Reserved.

This book or parts thereof may not be reproduced in any form, stored in any retrieval system, or transmitted in any form by any means—electronic, mechanical, photocopy, recording, or otherwise—without prior written permission of the Publisher

Color Test Page

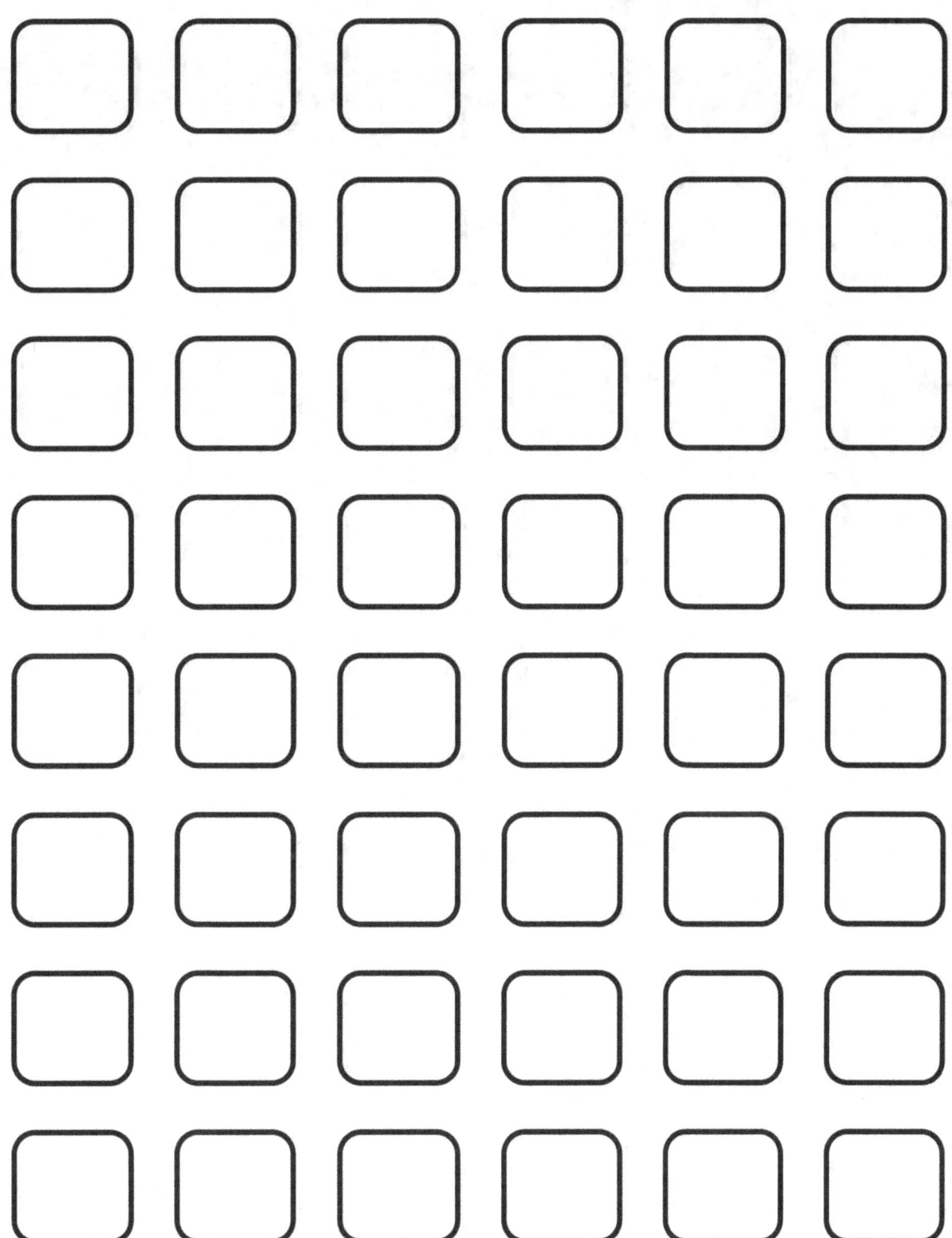

Color Test Page

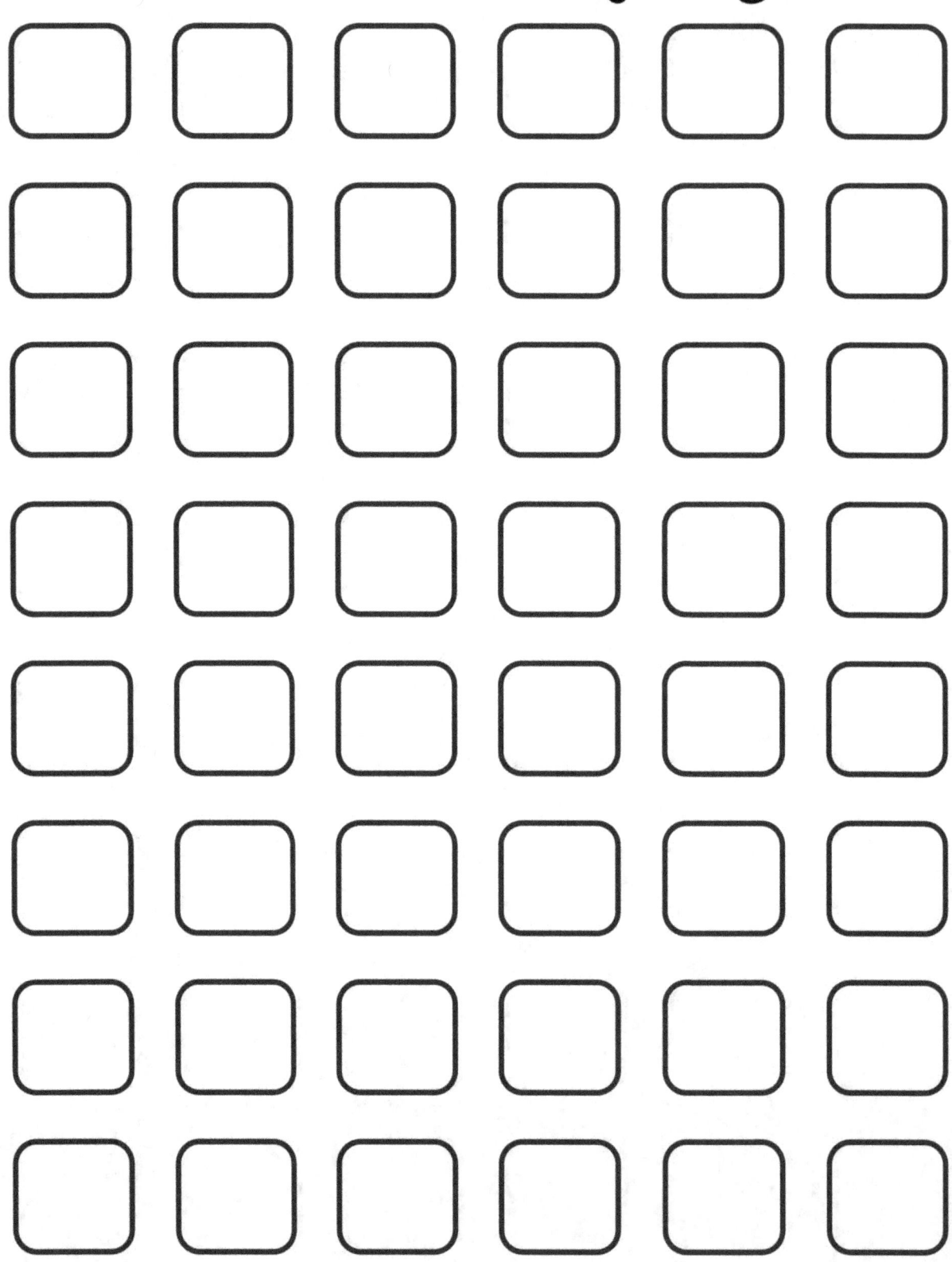

www.ingramcontent.com/pod-product-compliance
Lightning Source LLC
Chambersburg PA
CBHW062339220526
45469CB00008B/2774